Color the picture

Look at the pictures and find the 5 differences

How safe should babies, toddlers, children and adults travel safely? Match the right pictures

Go through the maze and see which way the boy was going to school

Color the picture and draw a reflection for each child.

Emma is going on a trip. What items should she take with her to feel safe? Surround them with a red circle.

Go through the maze and see which way the children were going home..

Look at the pictures which are safe and which are dangerous for your children to play. Draw a suitable smiley for each of the games. Sad - dangerous fun. Smiling - safe fun.

Check who is traveling safely and following the rules. Cross out incorrect behavior that could lead to a dangerous situation.

Look at the pictures and draw a smiling face where the pedestrian actually passes.

Help Katie cross the street. Number the pictures in the correct order.

Color the picture according to the numbers.

1 - yellow 2- red 3- green 4- blue 5- pink
6- black 7- brown

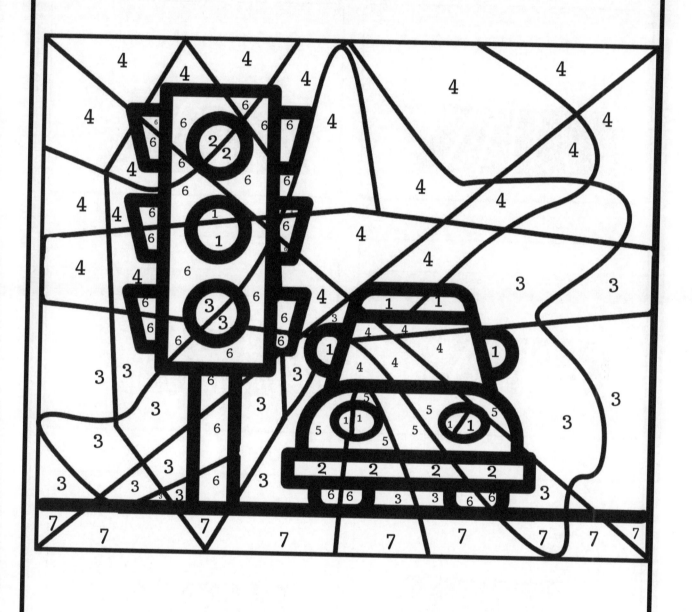

Look at the pictures. Draw out the mismatched pictures so that they show the correct crossing to the other side of the street.

Look at the pictures. Which road signs belong to the information signs group? Wrap them in a blue loop.

Not everyone is careful and safe at this junction. Put a red loop around those who are not acting properly.

Emergency services play a very important role in the everyday life of every person. They save lives and keep the roads safe. Each emergency service has its representative. Combine cars properly with the right profession.

Design your glare. You can give one of them to someone close.

Mark on the drawing the parts of the bicycle that must be in working order to ensure safety.

Find 3 helmets, 3 reflectors and 1 horn in the picture. Color the picture.

Look at the picture. Why is it crossed out? If you don't know, ask your parent to explain. Color the picture.

Look at the picture. Check if every child has a reflector?
Count the glare and enter the correct number.

Connect the vehicles with the appropriate signs with a line.

BUS STOP

CONSTRUCTION ZONE

DO NOT ENTER

Take a look at road signs. Arrange the shapes correctly.
Indicate the places where these signs are located.

Look at the pictures. Point out where the children are actually playing. The letters from the right pictures will form the password.

Remind Tom how to safely cross over to the other side. Color the picture.

Connect the lines. Then you will learn what rescue vehicle is hiding. Name it and indicate to which interventions it rides. Ask a parent for an emergency number. Please enter it below.

DIPLOMA

DIPLOMA

DIPLOMA

DIPLOMA

DIPLOMA

DIPLOMA

DIPLOMA

DIPLOMA

DIPLOMA

DIPLOMA

DIPLOMA

If you have completed all the tasks, you already know the rules of safe travel. Ask your parent to print you a diploma.

DIPLOMA

FOR SAFE PARTICIPANT OF THE ROAD TRAFFIC RECEIVES

....
....

Printed in Poland
by Amazon Fulfillment
Poland Sp. z o.o., Wrocław

38758375R00020